LET'S GO MARCHING!

Written by Judy Spevack   Illustrated by Lane Yerkes

Let's go marching.
There's so much to see.

I'm watching them.
And they're looking at me!

I see a bat, a cap, a dog.
I see a flag, a goat, a hog.

I see a jet, a kite, a hat.
I see a lion on a mat.

I see a mouse. I see a nose.
I see a queen. I see a rose.

I see a pan, a sun, a top.
I see a van, and a wet mop.

I see a box of yarn, and then, we pass the zoo and start again.